"Paper"
Through the Ages

"PAPER"
Through the Ages

by Shaaron Cosner
pictures by Priscilla Kiedrowski

Carolrhoda Books•Minneapolis, Minnesota

To Casey

Manufactured in the United States of America

Library of Congress Cataloging in Publication Data

Cosner, Shaaron.
    "Paper" through the ages.

    (A Carolrhoda on my own book)
    Summary: Describes the various types of surfaces that
have been used for writing throughout the ages includ-
ing cave walls, clay, wax, papyrus, and finally paper,
which was invented in China in the year 105.
    1. Paper—Juvenile literature. 2. Writing—
Materials and instruments—Juvenile literature.
[1. Paper. 2. Writing—Materials and instruments—
Juvenile literature] I. Kiedrowski, Priscilla, ill.
II. Title.
TS1105.5.C67   1984   001.54'3   84-7760
ISBN 0-87614-270-6 (lib. bdg.)

1 2 3 4 5 6 7 8 9 10 92 91 90 89 88 87 86 85 84

CONTENTS

New Words. 6

Stone. 11

Clay. 15

Papyrus. 19

Wax. 25

Parchment. 29

Paper. 33

Tricks with Paper. 46

NEW WORDS

Some of the words in this story may be new to you. They are printed in **bold type** the first time they come up in the story. Here is what they mean and how to say them.

invent (in-VENT): to make something for the first time. Thomas Edison *invented* the light bulb. Ts'ai Lun *invented* paper.

cavemen (KAVE-men): a nickname for people who lived in caves over 15,000 years ago

tablet (TAB-lut): a flat piece of stone, metal, or clay that can be used to write on

hieroglyphics (hy-ruh-GLIF-ix): the ancient Egyptian way of writing

papyrus (puh-PIE-rus): a tall, reedy plant that grows along the Nile River in Egypt; also the writing material that is made from that plant

parchment (PARCH-munt): an animal skin that has been worked on so that people can write on it

pulp (puhlp): a material made from wood or rags that is used to make paper

waterproof (WAW-tur-proof): able to shed water. A *waterproof* coat will keep you dry when it rains.

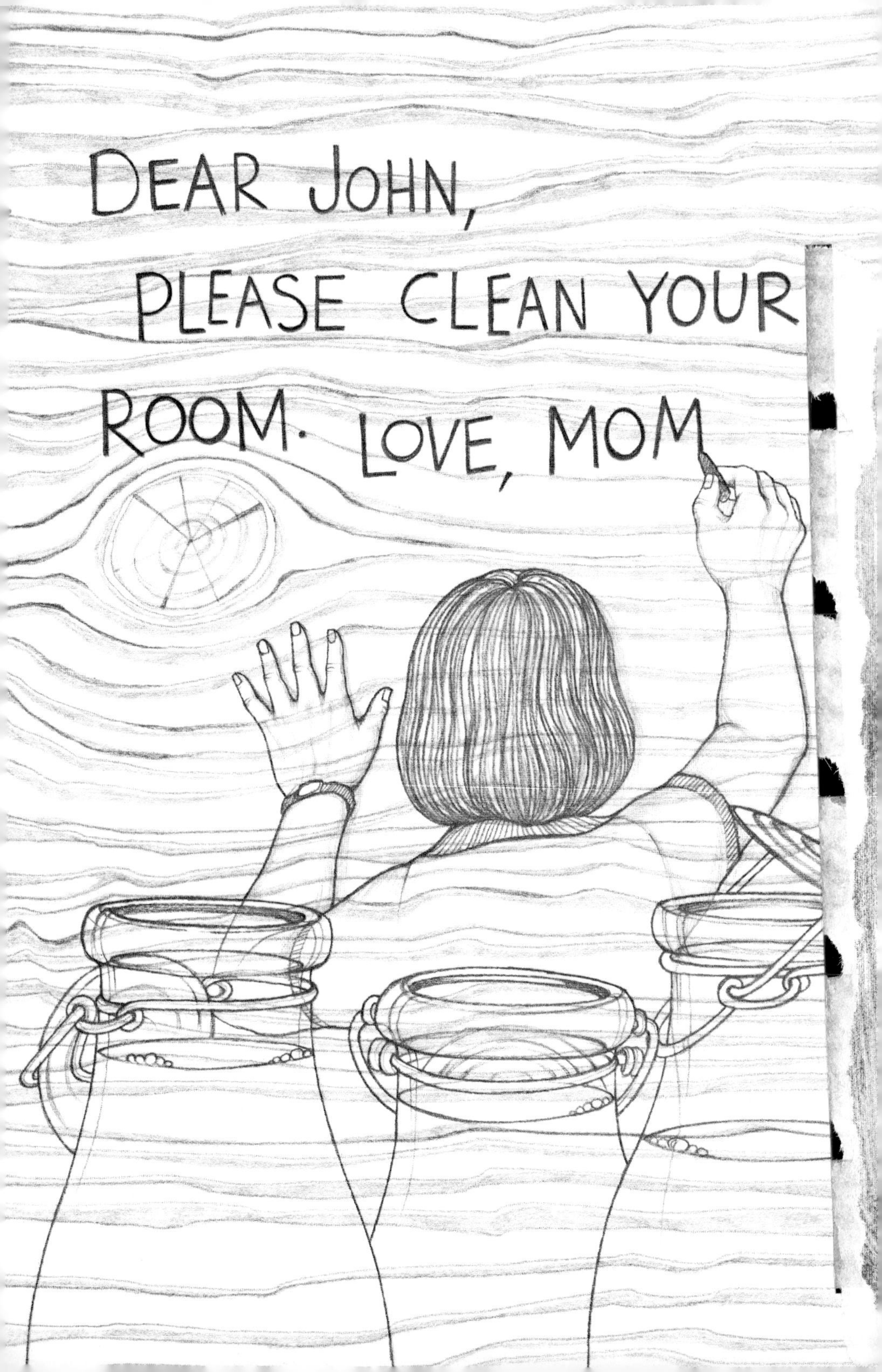
DEAR JOHN,
PLEASE CLEAN YOUR ROOM. LOVE, MOM

Where would we be without paper?

Would milk come only in bottles?

Would we write letters on walls?

Would this book be made of wood?

Paper was **invented**

about 1,800 years ago.

But people who looked like us

have been around

for over 30,000 years.

What were they writing on?

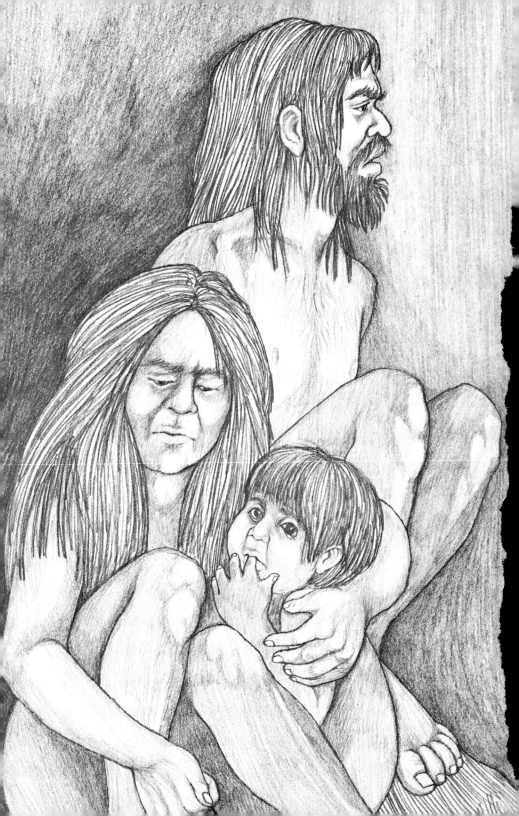

STONE

You may have heard stories
about **cavemen**.
These people lived
over 15,000 years ago.
They had no alphabet,
so they could not write.
But they could paint pictures.

They painted on their cave walls.
They made brushes from animal hair.
They made paint
from dirt and animal fat.

Most of their pictures show animals.
Some can still be seen today.
They tell us something about
how these people lived.

CLAY

For thousands of years
people used stone for paper.
Then, about 5,000 years ago,
people in the land of Sumer
came up with something better.

The Sumerians had
a kind of picture alphabet.
They could write.
But writing in stone is hard work.

So the Sumerians made clay **tablets**.
They wrote on wet clay.
Then they dried the clay in the sun
until it got hard.

PAPYRUS

The Egyptians had
a kind of picture alphabet too.
You may have heard of it.
It is called **hieroglyphics**.
Each picture stood for
a sound or an idea.

As time went on,
more people learned to write.
But carrying around
stone or clay tablets
was heavy work!
People needed something lighter.
About 4,000 years ago
the Egyptians found it.
They learned to make
something like paper from plants.
The plant they used is called **papyrus**.
Our word paper comes from it.

The Egyptians cut the papyrus
into thin strips.
They laid the strips side by side.
Then they laid another layer
across the first.
They covered both layers
with mud or paste.
Then they pressed them together.
When the mud or paste dried,
the papyrus stuck together.
It was stiff
and it smelled terrible,
but people could write on it.
It is called papyrus too.

WAX

The Greeks and Romans
came up with another way
to make writing easier.
They covered wood tablets with wax.
Then they wrote in the wax.

People could use these tablets
over and over again.
They just rubbed off the words.
Then they put on new wax.
Sometimes they tied
the tablets together
to make a book.
Later the Greeks and Romans
began to use papyrus.
Later still, they used **parchment**.

PARCHMENT

About 2,200 years ago,
people in the city of Pergamum
had a problem.
They had been using papyrus
for paper.
But the Egyptians were afraid
that the Pergamum library
was getting better
than the best library in Egypt.
They would not let Pergamum
have any more papyrus.

The people of Pergamum
would have to find something new.
They did.
They found parchment.

Parchment is made from animal skins.
First the hair and fat are taken off.
Then the skin is stretched and scraped.
Finally it is softened.

Parchment was very strong.
It was easy to fold.
People liked it better than papyrus.
They liked it so much
that they went on using it
for 2,200 years!
We still use some parchment today.

PAPER

In the year 105,
a Chinese man named Ts'ai Lun
boiled wood strips in water.
Then he beat the mixture
until it was mushy.
Today this mush is called **pulp**.

Ts'ai Lun built a frame.
He stretched cloth over it.
Then he dipped the frame
into the pulp.
When he lifted it,
the cloth held a thin layer of pulp.
The water dripped out
through the cloth.
Ts'ai Lun dried and pressed
his layer of pulp.
What was left?
Paper!
Ts'ai Lun had invented paper!

The Chinese people
loved this new paper.
They soon thought
of many ways to use it.
Before long,
people were using toilet paper.
They wiped their faces
with paper napkins.

They loved paper so much,
they tried to keep it a secret.
But the secret got out.
Soon people in Korea
were making paper windows.

People in Japan made paper bags,
lanterns, and coats.

The Japanese learned
to cover their paper with oil.
This made it **waterproof**.
Now they could use it for umbrellas!

The Japanese even made houses
out of paper.
Each room had one or two
thin paper walls.

The paper let the light shine in.
If it got dirty,
it could be taken down.
New paper could go up.

People in China, Japan, and Korea
knew a lot about paper.
They found that they could use
old rags to make paper too.
But it took hundreds of years
for the rest of the world
to learn about paper.
Maya Indians in Central America
had to invent
their own kind of paper.
They pounded it out of tree bark.
They lived too far away
to hear about Ts'ai Lun.

Paper has come a long way
since Ts'ai Lun.
Today it is made by machines
as long as a city block.
One machine makes 500 miles
of paper each day!
Paper can be made to last
for 400,000 years!
Today there are over 7,000
different kinds of paper.
The United States alone
makes over 60,000,000 tons
of paper each year.
Everywhere we look, there's paper.
Paper stamps. Paper towels.
Paper cups. Paper everywhere.
What would we do without it?

Tricks with Paper

$1 + 1 = 1?$

It does when you try to cut this magic loop in two. This trick will make your friends want to take extra arithmetic lessons.

First make your magic loop where no one can see you. Cut out a long strip of newspaper about 3 inches wide. Twist over one end of the newspaper and then glue or tape the ends together. This special twist is what makes the trick work.

Now you are ready to trick your friends. Poke a hole in the strip and begin to cut the loop lengthwise down the middle. Ask your friends how many loops you'll have after you've finished cutting. "Two," they will say. Just smile. Right before you've finished say, "Alli babba, babba shizzam, not two loops but one I am!" And sure enough, when you have finished cutting, one large loop will open up, not two smaller ones!

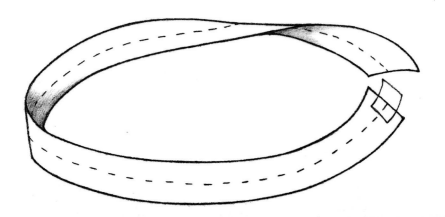

Now you <u>don't</u> see it, now you do!

Did you ever want to send a note to someone that no one else could read? You would have had a hard time if all you had to write on was stone! But today it's easy. Here's how.

You'll need a small brush, a bowl or a glass, and a piece of paper. You'll also need any one of these liquids: lemon or onion juice, a little sugar mixed in water, or milk. Put the liquid into your bowl or glass. Then dip your brush into it and write a message on the piece of paper. No one can see it. But hold it near a hot light bulb and the writing will show up as if by magic.